T 2534

656
GNP

Pebble® Plus

Pet Questions and Answers

DOGS

Questions and Answers

by Christina Mia Gardeski

CAPSTONE PRESS
a capstone imprint

Pebble Plus is published by Capstone Press,
1710 Roe Crest Drive, North Mankato, Minnesota 56003
www.mycapstone.com

Library of Congress Cataloging-in-Publication Data
Cataloging-in-Publication data is on file with the Library of Congress.
ISBN 978-1-5157-0355-6 (library binding)
ISBN 978-1-5157-0362-4 (paperback)
ISBN 978-1-5157-0368-6 (eBook PDF)

Editorial Credits
Carrie Braulick Sheely and Alesha Halvorson, editors; Kayla Rossow, designer;
Pam Mitsakos, media researcher; Gene Bentdahl, production specialist

Photo Credits
Shutterstock: Andresr, 9, anetapics, 11, AVAVA, 13, Bobbymne, 15, Javier Brosch, 5,
Ksenia Raykova, cover, l i g h t p o e t, 7, MaKars, 1, 22, Monkey Business Images, 19,
SomPhoto, 21; Thinkstock: Fuse, 17

Note to Parents and Teachers

The Pet Questions and Answers set supports national curriculum standards for science related
to life science. This book describes and illustrates dogs. The images support early readers in
understanding the text. The repetition of words and phrases helps early readers learn new
words. This book also introduces early readers to subject-specific vocabulary words, which are
defined in the Glossary section. Early readers may need assistance to read some words and
to use the Table of Contents, Glossary, Read More, Internet Sites, Critical Thinking Using the
Common Core, and Index sections of the book.

Printed in China.
022016   007713

Table of Contents

Who Waits By the Door?

My dog!

Dogs have twice as many ear muscles as people. This helps them hear sounds people cannot hear. They know someone is at the door before anyone even knocks.

Why Do Dogs Bark?

Dogs bark to tell people and other dogs what they want. They bark to tell people they want to eat or walk.

They bark at other dogs when they play.

Dogs also bark to say stay away.

Do Dogs Get Lonely?

Dogs like to be with people and other dogs. Most wild dogs live in packs. A pet dog's human family is like its pack. Dogs do not like to be alone.

Why Do Dogs Wag Their Tails?

Dogs wag their tails to tell how they feel. Happy dogs often wag their tails high and to the right.

Dogs with tails wagging low and to the left might be upset.

What Do Dogs Eat?

Dogs will eat most foods if you let them. But some food for people can make dogs sick. Wet or dry dog food that is high in protein is best.

They also need fresh water every day.

Do Dogs Work?

Some dogs have special jobs.

Police dogs track down law breakers.

Others find people who are lost

or hurt. Some dogs help people who

cannot see.

Does My Dog Need a Check-Up?

Healthy dogs get check-ups every year. A vet checks the dog from head to tail. The vet listens to its heart and lungs. The vet makes sure the dog does not have fleas or ticks.

Can I Let My Dog Outside?

Dogs love the outdoors.

A fence can keep your dog safe

in the yard. Take it for walks

on a leash each day. Never

leave your dog alone outside.

Why Do Dogs Sniff Everything?

Dogs sniff to learn. Some dogs can smell if people are sick.

Their wet noses know where you were and what you touched.

Glossary

flea—a tiny, jumping insect that sucks blood

leash—a strap for holding and walking an animal

muscle—a part of the body that helps move, lift, or push

pack—a group of animals that hunts together

protein—part of food that builds strong bones and muscles

tick—an insect that attaches itself to a person or animal to suck blood

vet—a doctor who cares for animals, short for veterinarian

Read More

Murray, Julie. *Dogs.* Family Pets. Minneapolis, Minn.: ABDO Kids, 2015.

Rustad, Martha E.H. *Dogs.* Little Scientist. Mankato, Minn.: Capstone Press, 2015.

Shores, Erika L. *Pet Dogs Up Close.* Pets Up Close. Mankato, Minn.: Capstone Press, 2015.

Internet Sites

FactHound offers a safe, fun way to find Internet sites related to this book. All of the sites on FactHound have been researched by our staff.

Here's all you do:

Visit *www.facthound.com*

Type in this code: 9781515703556

Super-cool stuff!

Check out projects, games and lots more at **www.capstonekids.com**

Critical Thinking
Using the Common Core

1. Why is it important to take your dog to the vet for regular check-ups? (Key Ideas and Details)

2. Why might a dog bark at someone? (Key Ideas and Details)

Index